TROPICAL FISH LOOK-AND-LEARN

by
MARY E. SWEENEY

Photographs: Dr. Herbert R. Axelrod, B. A. Branson, K. L. Chew, D. Conkel, J. Elias, S. Franke, Gan Fish Farm, R. Goldstein, H. Grier, B. Kahl, E. Kennedy, A. Kochetov, H. Linke, H. Mayland, A. Norman, J.Palicka, R. Pethiyagoda, MP & C. Piednoir, H.-J. Richter, A. Roth, S. Sane, W. Sommer, M. Smith, E. Taylor, K. Tanaka, J. Vierke, World Wide Fish Farm, M. Yamamoto, L. W. Yat, R. Zukal

Distributed in the UNITED STATES to the Pet Trade by T.F.H. Publications, Inc., One T.F.H. Plaza, Neptune City, NJ 07753; distributed in the UNITED STATES to the Bookstore and Library Trade by National Book Network, Inc. 4720 Boston Way, Lanham MD 20706; in CANADA to the Pet Trade by H & L Pet Supplies Inc., 27 Kingston Crescent, Kitchener, Ontario N2B 2T6; Rolf C. Hagen Ltd., 3225 Sartelon Street, Montreal 382 Quebec; in CANADA to the Book Trade by Macmillan of Canada (A Division of Canada Publishing Corporation), 164 Commander Boulevard, Agincourt, Ontario M1S 3C7; in the United Kingdom by T.F.H. Publications, PO Box 15, Waterlooville PO7 6BQ; in AUSTRALIA AND THE SOUTH PACIFIC by T.F.H. (Australia), Pty. Ltd., Box 149, Brookvale 2100 N.S.W., Australia; in NEW ZEALAND by Brooklands Aquarium Ltd. 5 McGiven Drive, New Plymouth, RD1 New Zealand; in Japan by T.F.H. Publications, Japan—Jiro Tsuda, 10-12-3 Ohjidai, Sakura, Chiba 285, Japan; in SOUTH AFRICA by Multipet Pty. Ltd., P.O. Box 35347, Northway, 4065, South Africa. Published by T.F.H. Publications, Inc.
Manufactured in the United States of America by T.F.H. Publications, Inc.

SUGGESTED READING

YF-100, 32 pages

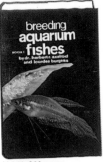

TS-139, 144 pages
Over 240 color photos

H-946, 320 pages
188 color photos

H-963, 320 pages
161 color photos

H-966, 448 pages
244 color photos

CO-002S, 128 pages
88 color photos

CO-003S, 128 pages
83 color photos

SK-033, 64 pages
Over 50 color photos

TU-016, 64 pages
93 color photos

H-1077, over 1150 pages
Over 7000 color photos

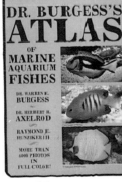

H-1100, 736 pages
Over 4000 color photos

TS-104, 192 pages

E-701, 32 pages
20 color photos

TT-026, 208 pages
Over 200 color photos

CO-007S, 128 pages
180 color photos

H-1097, 800 pages
Over 1700 color photos

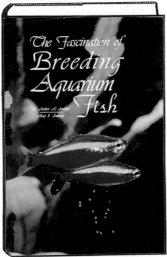

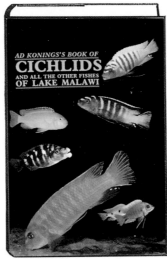

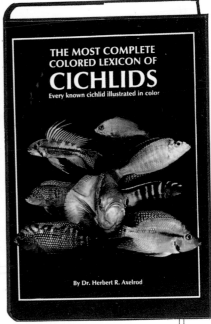

TS-185, 448 pages
Over 980 color photos

TS-157, 448 pages
Over 1000 color photos

TS-190, 864 pages
Over 2250 color photos

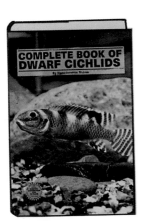

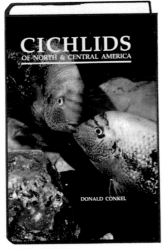

TS-121, 208 pages
Over 400 photos

TS-184, 192 pages
Over 250 color photos

TS-116, 500 pages   Over 600 color photos

CO-011S, 128 pp.
148 photos

TS-118, 160 pages
175 color photos

H-945, 382 pages

T.F.H. Publications
One T.F.H. Plaza
Third & Union Avenues
Neptune, NJ 07753

These and thousands of other animal books have been published by T.F.H. T.F.H. is the world's largest publisher of animal books. You can find our titles at the same place you bought this one, or write to us for a free catalog.

INTRODUCTION

When you start your first aquarium and find that you can keep beautifully colored tropical fishes happy and healthy, you have started a journey, the rewards of which cannot be measured by any standard yardstick. This is a hobby that will give you countless hours filled with fascinating observations. You will find that your imagination and your aquarium will take you to warm and wonderful places all over the globe as you learn more about your fishes, their habits, behaviors, and natural habitats. You will have the opportunity to observe firsthand a genuine miracle when your fishes present you with tiny fry. Most of all, if you haven't met him already, you will discover the natural scientist within yourself—the aquarist.

It is not difficult to set up an aquarium. Your pet shop has everything you need to get started—books, starter kits, tanks, filters, heaters...fishes. Just about all you have to do is add water. The most important

◀ Power filters are excellent for keeping your water in pristine condition. In addition to scouring the water of floating particles, the biological activity in the chamber will cleanse the water of toxic wastes. Photo courtesy of Hagen.

For the beginner, a quality starter kit includes all the necessary equipment. Photo courtesy of Hagen. ▶

elements in tropical fishkeeping are the water, heater, filter, and tank. If kept in good, clean water of the right temperature and chemistry, most fishes will thrive (provided they have good food). The filter and regular water changes will keep the water fresh and sweet. The heater will keep the water the right temperature for tropicals. The tank, of course, will contain the clean, warmed water that will contain the fishes.

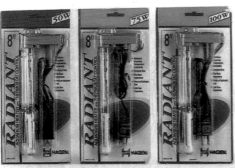

▲ All tropical aquaria require heaters. Even if you live in a warm climate, cool nights could lead to chilling of the fishes. Photo courtesy of Hagen.

The scope and variety of aquarium products is awesome. There is no reason that everyone can't have the aquarium of their dreams. Photo courtesy of Hagen.

Wet-dry filtration is used with tremendous success in the saltwater side of the hobby. Units are now becoming available for the freshwater hobbyist as well. Photo courtesy of Hagen.

There are air pumps for every purpose under water. No matter what type of filtration you use, you will find that an air pump will be handy to have. You can use them with extra filters and aerators. You never know when you are going to need extra air for your fishes. Photo courtesy of Hagen. ▼

Accessories like lights and hoods are useful...the hoods keep jumping fish from jumping out and the lights are handy for viewing fishes and necessary for growing plants.

As you grow with your aquarium, you will naturally want to customize it to your personal taste. Each person has their own interpretation of how an

◄ A thermometer is an essential piece of equipment. Your finger is just not accurate enough to gauge the temperature of the water for tropical fishes. Photo courtesy of Hagen.

▲ A "species tank" that contains only one kind of fish can be delightful. This gives the aquarist the opportunity to study the chosen species in great detail.

aquarium should look, and even using the same plants, rocks, driftwood, and decorations, no two aquaria ever look exactly the same.

When selecting your fishes, bear in mind that they will probably be youngsters that will grow quickly. If you are careful not to overstock the tank, your fishes and your filter will both have an opportunity to mature. If, like so many of us, you buy every fish you like, you will probably suffer heavy losses until the tank stabilizes. A good aquarium book like *Tropical Fish as a Hobby* (TFH TT-017) will give you step-by-step instructions on everything you need to know to get started.

▲ Nitrifying bacteria from a bottle will help get your aquarium filtering system up and running at peak efficiency in the least possible amount of time. Photo courtesy of Hagen.

▲ Internal power filters can be an excellent choice, especially when you don't have a lot of room for an outside filter. They are attractive and functional. Photo courtesy of Hagen.

A gravel washer is a wonderful ▶ device that cleans your gravel and removes the dirty water at the same time. Photo courtesy of Hagen.

AMAZING ANABANTOIDS

Anabantoids are generally gentle fishes—except for some rivalry between males—and on the whole are very amenable, excellent members of a peaceful community aquarium. They love warm water and will show their finest colors and manners when kept at around 80°F. Filtration of their water is not strictly necessary, but if you have a tendency to overstock or overfeed the tank, it is best to use a filter to make sure the water is kept clean. They do not like strong currents and soon become exhausted if they are not able to escape into calmer water. Plants are abundant in their native Asian waters and an important item in the anabantoid aquarium. The pH and hardness of the water is not important, but aged water is. This means that you should take care to change only very small amounts of water in an established aquarium.

Anabantoids have small, upturned mouths. They like all manner of small insects and worms, preferably floating on the top of the water or on the leaves of plants. They will feast on brine shrimp, tubifex, whiteworms, and bloodworms, but will readily accept prepared aquarium foods for their staple diet. Variety is very important, as is restraint from overfeeding.

◀ A male Betta meets another male Betta with a great show of fins and flaring of gills—even when it's only his own reflection in the glass.

▶

Betta splendens, wild type. This is what the "real" Betta looks like. Is it any wonder that the Betta is one of the most popular of aquarium fishes?

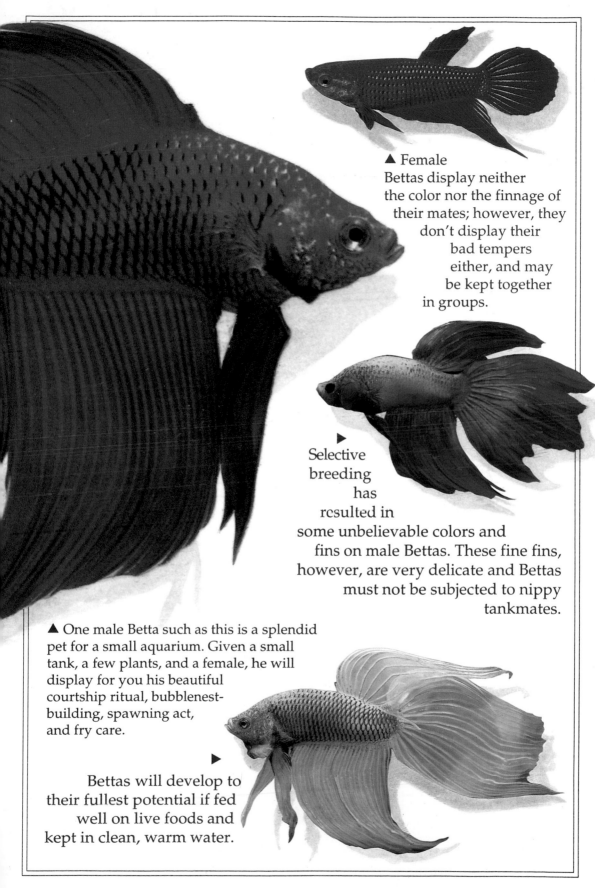

▲ Female
Bettas display neither
the color nor the finnage of
their mates; however, they
don't display their
bad tempers
either, and may
be kept together
in groups.

►
Selective
breeding
has
resulted in
some unbelievable colors and
fins on male Bettas. These fine fins,
however, are very delicate and Bettas
must not be subjected to nippy
tankmates.

▲ One male Betta such as this is a splendid
pet for a small aquarium. Given a small
tank, a few plants, and a female, he will
display for you his beautiful
courtship ritual, bubblenest-
building, spawning act,
and fry care.

►
Bettas will develop to
their fullest potential if fed
well on live foods and
kept in clean, warm water.

Most anabantoids are bubblenest builders. The male blows bubbles of air and "spit," creating a nest that holds together very well in the still waters preferred by anabantoids. After the spawning act is completed, the male will tend the eggs in the bubblenest, constantly working around the nest and blowing ever more bubbles until the eggs begin to hatch into wrigglers. As the tiny fry fall out of the nest, the male tenderly picks them up in his mouth and returns them to the nest until they are free swimming.

▲ The Claret Betta (*Betta coccina*) is one of the beautiful bubblenest builders that the anabantoid enthusiast can add to his collection. During breeding, the colors intensify remarkably, making this peaceful species well worth a place in the aquarium.

▲ The Kalimantan Betta (*Betta foerschi*). With bubblenest builders, the male wraps his body around the female and fertilizes the eggs as she releases them.

The Striped Betta (*Betta fasciata*) explodes with blue iridescence during courtship and breeding. ▶

The Croaking Gourami (*Trichopsis vittatus*) blows bubbles to make its nest. When the fish spawn, the eggs float up into the bubblenest where they are tended by the male for the 36-hour incubation period. ▶

▲ The Crescent Betta (*Betta imbellis*) is fond of heavily planted tanks and will show its best colors and behavior in such a tank. This is a relatively peaceful Betta and can be kept easily in a community arrangement.

▲ The Paradisefish (*Macropodus opercularis*) was one of the first tropical fishes ever kept in the aquarium. It was imported to France from China in 1869 and was an immediate hit. Both males and females are quite aggressive; however, their good looks still make them desirable aquarium fish.

The Brunei Beauty (*Betta macrostoma*) is a mouthbrooder and the *male* carries the ▼ eggs!

Anabantoids are also called labyrinthfishes. The labyrinth is a special organ that allows them to breathe air from the surface of the oxygen-poor waters of their Asian homelands. This ability is a distinct advantage in nature, where they are found in shallow ditches, rice paddies, stagnant pools...wherever.

The labyrinth organ is very sensitive to chilling when it is developing in the fry and they should be kept in warm, covered tanks.

▲ The Honey Gourami (*Colisa chuna*) sports a dark blue to black throat that intensifies during courtship. They are very peaceful and shy and really appreciate a sunny, planted tank with quiet water.

◄ The Giant Gourami (*Colisa fasciata*) is not really all that big at 4 to 5 inches. Give them a warm, well-planted tank that is not disturbed often and they will surprise you with the number of fry they produce! They are a little shy when first brought home, but will become very lively as they adjust to the new conditions.

►
The Three-Spot Gourami (*Trichogaster trichopterus*) in its gold form. The more common blue morph is an exceptionally beautiful two-toned navy and light blue fish. This is a lively, richly colored fish that is gregarious and very easily bred. The males are slightly territorial at breeding time, but only to repel invaders. Provide a warm, planted tank and good food and soon you will have several generations coexisting in harmony.

The Pearl Gourami (*Trichogaster leeri*) builds a bubblenest among the fine-leaved plants floating at the water's surface. Both the males and females are beautifully colored with red, silver, and blue. This is an easy fish to keep provided it is gently handled and well fed. Some fine-leaved plants, a little warmth, some peaceful tankmates, and you will find the Pearl Gourami blossoming into a lively, inquisitive fish. ▲

◄ Dwarf Gouramis are small, about 2 to 3 inches. The males are most colorful. The females are somewhat paler with more rounded fins. There are several color varieties and even long-finned types.

▲ The Chocolate Gourami (*Sphaerichthys osphromenoides*) is one of the mouthbrooding species of anabantoid. It will do very well in the aquarium provided there is adequate heat. Chilling is disastrous so keep the water at about 82°F for best results.

◄

The Dwarf Gourami (*Colisa lalia*) is one of the greatest aquarium fish going...hardy, easy to feed, peaceful, and gorgeous!

COOL CATFISHES

The miniature catfishes of the *Corydoras*, *Brochis*, and *Aspidoras* genera are the adorables of the aquarium with their delicate whiskers, saucy little winks, and generally comical demeanor. They have very easygoing personalities and are flexible about aquarium conditions. Relying on their sensitive barbels to locate their food, Corys spend most of their time "whiskering" every part of the aquarium. They are hungry little fellows and need to be kept well fed to maintain good condition.

Corydoras barbatus is an unusual species, one of the prettiest and largest of the Corys. Mature males sometimes develop bristles on their heads.
▶

Aspidoras pauciradiatus is a peaceful schooling species that is suitable for species tanks or community tanks with "safe" fishes. *Aspidoras* species appreciate small live foods in addition to their regular diet. ▶

◀ There have been no reported spawnings of *Corydoras axelrodi* in the aquarium. Be the first and become a part of aquarium history.

◄ *Corydoras panda* was named after the popular Chinese panda "bear" for the black eye stripe. Among the most popular of the Corys, Pandas like good clean water and the company of their fellows.

▲ *Corydoras ambiacus* is a native of Peru and a friendly species that does best in small groups. They prefer extremely soft water and a dark sand substrate.

◄ *Corydoras guapore* was first collected by the famous explorer Harald Schultz. It is an active, nimble fish in the aquarium and should have enough open swimming space.

Brochis britskii is a prize for any aquarist. The iridescent green and orangish coloration and large body size makes this an outstanding fish.
▶

▲ *Corydoras aeneus* is very easy to keep and breed. They come from shallow waters with low oxygen content. Because of this, they sometimes rely on intestinal respiration and can be seen dashing to the surface for a mouthful of air. Aeneus is the most popular of all the Corys in the aquarium hobby.

Loricariids, or suckermouth catfishes, are found in a wide variety of habitats ranging from soft, acidic water in marshes to fast-moving mountain creeks. They like to stay near the banks and sometimes dig little caves in the muddy banks. Most Loricariid species are nocturnal and spend their nights roaming in search of food.

▶ Unusual catfishes like this *Pseudacanthicus* sp. are often imported from South America and kept in aquaria, but little is known about them from a scientific standpoint.

▲ *Hypostomus* sp., or Plecos, need plenty of vegetables in their diets. Vegetable-based flake foods, boiled and raw spinach, parboiled zucchini, boiled oatmeal, even rabbit pellets will satisfy these requirements.

▼ The genus *Pterygoplichthys* contains about 20 species coming mostly from Paraguay, Brazil, and Peru. Loricariids are highly territorial amongst themselves, but very peaceful with other fishes.